TH[illegible]
FLAVIUS JOSEPHUS

FLAVIUS JOSEPHUS

AETERNA PRESS

PUBLISHED BY AETERNA PRESS.
COVER DESIGN BY AETERNA PRESS.

ISBN-13: 978-1-78516-733-1

AVAILABLE AS AN E-BOOK:
WWW.AETERNAPRESS.COM

CONTENTS

The Life Of Flavius Josephus

1. THE family from which I am derived is not an ignoble one, but hath descended all along from the priests; and as nobility among several people is of a different origin, so with us to be of the sacerdotal dignity, is an indication of the splendor of a family. Now, I am not only sprung from a sacerdotal family in general, but from the first of the twenty-four courses; and as among us there is not only a considerable difference between one family of each course and another, I am of the chief family of that first course also; nay, further, by my mother I am of the royal blood; for the children of Asamoneus, from whom that family was derived, had both the office of the high priesthood, and the dignity of a king, for a long time together. I will accordingly set down my progenitors in order. My grandfather's father was named Simon, with the addition of Psellus: he lived at the same time with that son of Simon the high priest, who first of all the high priests was named Hyrcanus. This Simon Psellus had nine sons, one of whom was Matthias, called Ephlias: he married the daughter of Jonathan the high priest, which Jonathan was the first of the sons of Asamoneus, who was high priest, and was the brother of Simon the high priest also. This Matthias had a son called Matthias Curtus, and that in the first year of the government of Hyrcanus: his son's name was Joseph, born in the ninth year of the reign of Alexandra: his son Matthias was born in the tenth year of the reign of Archclaus; as was I born to Matthias in the first year of the reign of Caius Caesar. I have three sons: Hyrcanus, the eldest, was born in the fourth year of the reign of Vespasian, as was Justus born in the seventh, and Agrippa in the ninth. Thus have I set down the genealog of my family as I have found it described in the public records, and so bid adieu to those who calumniate me [as of a lower original].

2. Now, my father Matthias was not only eminent on account of is nobility, but had a higher commendation on account of his righteousness, and was in great reputation in Jerusalem, the greatest city we have. I was myself brought up with my brother, whose name was Matthias, for he was my own

brother, by both father and mother; and I made mighty proficiency in the improvements of my learning, and appeared to have both a great memory and understanding. Moreover, when I was a child, and about fourteen years of age, I was commended by all for the love I had to learning; on which account the high priests and principal men of the city came then frequently to me together, in order to know my opinion about the accurate understanding of points of the law. And when I was about sixteen years old, I had a mind to make trim of the several sects that were among us. These sects are three: - The first is that of the Pharisees, the second that Sadducees, and the third that of the Essens, as we have frequently told you; for I thought that by this means I might choose the best, if I were once acquainted with them all; so I contented myself with hard fare, and underwent great difficulties, and went through them all. Nor did I content myself with these trials only; but when I was informed that one, whose name was Banus, lived in the desert, and used no other clothing than grew upon trees, and had no other food than what grew of its own accord, and bathed himself in cold water frequently, both by night and by day, in order to preserve his chastity, I imitated him in those things, and continued with him three years. So when I had accomplished my desires, I returned back to the city, being now nineteen years old, and began to conduct myself according to the rules of the sect of the Pharisees, which is of kin to the sect of the Stoics, as the Greeks call them.

3. But when I was in the twenty-sixth year of my age, it happened that I took a voyage to Rome, and this on the occasion which I shall now describe. At the time when Felix was procurator of Judea there were certain priests of my acquaintance, and very excellent persons they were, whom on a small and trifling occasion he had put into bonds, and sent to Rome to plead their cause before Caesar. These I was desirous to procure deliverance for, and that especially because I was informed that they were not unmindful of piety towards God, even under their afflictions, but supported themselves with figs and nuts. Accordingly I came to Rome, though it were through a great number of hazards by sea; for as our ship was drowned in the Adriatic Sea, we that were in it, being about six hundred in number, swam for our lives all the night; when, upon the first appearance of the day, and upon our sight of a ship of Cyrene, I and some others, eighty in all, by God's providence, prevented the rest, and were taken up into the other ship. And when I had thus escaped, and was come to Dieearchia, which the Italians call Puteoli, I became acquainted with Aliturius, an actor of plays, and much beloved by Nero, but a Jew by birth; and through his interest became known to Poppea, Caesar's wife, and took care, as soon as possible, to entreat her to procure that the priests might be set

at liberty. And when, besides this favor, I had obtained many presents from Poppea, I returned home again.

4. And now I perceived innovations were already begun, and that there were a great many very much elevated in hopes of a revolt from the Romans. I therefore endeavored to put a stop to these tumultuous persons, and persuaded them to change their minds; and laid before their eyes against whom it was that they were going to fight, and told them that they were inferior to the Romans not only in martial skill, but also in good fortune; and desired them not rashly, and after the most foolish manner, to bring on the dangers of the most terrible mischiefs upon their country, upon their families, and upon themselves. And this I said with vehement exhortation, because I foresaw that the end of such a war would be most unfortunate to us. But I could not persuade them; for the madness of desperate men was quite too hard for me.

5. I was then afraid, lest, by inculcating these things so often, I should incur their hatred and their suspicions, as if I were of our enemies' party, and should run into the danger of being seized by them, and slain; since they were already possessed of Antonia, which was the citadel; so I retired into the inner court of the temple. Yet did I go out of the temple again, after Manahem and the principal of the band of robbers were put to death, when I abode among the high priests and the chief of the Pharisees. But no small fear seized upon us when we saw the people in arms, while we ourselves knew not what we should do, and were not able to restrain the seditious. However, as the danger was directly upon us, we pretended that we were of the same opinion with them, but only advised them to be quiet for the present, and to let the enemy go away, still hoping that Gessius [Florus] would not be long ere he came, and that with great forces, and so put an end to these seditious proceedings.

6. But, upon his coming and fighting, he was beaten, and a great many of those that were with him fell. And this disgrace which Gessius [with Cestius] received, became the calamity of our whole nation; for those that were fond of the war were so far elevated with this success, that they had hopes of finally conquering the Romans. Of which war another occasion was ministered; which was this: - Those that dwelt in the neighboring cities of Syria seized upon such Jews as dwelt among them, with their wives and children, and slew them, when they had not the least occasion of complaint against them; for they did neither attempt any innovation or revolt from the Romans, nor had they given any marks of hatred or treacherous designs towards the Syrians. But what was done by the inhabitants of Scythopolis was the most impious and most highly criminal of all; for when the Jews their enemies came upon them from without, they forced the Jews that were among them to bear arms against their

own countrymen, which it is unlawful for us to do; and when, by their assistance, they had joined battle with those who attacked them, and had beaten them, after that victory they forgot the assurances they had given these their fellow citizens and confederates, and slew them all, being in number many ten thousands [13,000]. The like miseries were undergone by those Jews that were the inhabitants of Damascus. But we have given a more accurate account of these things in the books of the Jewish war. I only mention them now, because I would demonstrate to my readers, that the Jews' war with the Romans was not voluntary, but that, for the main, they were forced by necessity to enter into it.

7. So when Gessius had been beaten, as we have said already, the principal men of Jerusalem, seeing that the robbers and innovators had arms in great plenty, and fearing lest they, while they were unprovided of arms, should be in subjection to their enemies, which also came to be the case afterward; and, being informed that all Galilee had not yet revolted from the Romans, but that some part of it was still quiet; they sent me and two others of the priests, who were men of excellent characters, Joazar and Judas, in order to persuade the ill men there to lay down their arms, and to teach them this lesson, - That it were better to have those arms reserved for the most courageous men that the nation had [than to be kept there]; for that it had been resolved, That those our best men should always have their arms ready against futurity; but still so, that they should wait to see what the Romans would do.

8. When I had therefore received these instructions, I came into Galilee, and found the people of Sepphoris in no small agony about their country, by reason that the Galileans had resolved to plunder it, on account of the friendship they had with the Romans, and because they had given their right hand, and made a league with Cestius Gallus, the president of Syria. But I delivered them all out of the fear they were in, and persuaded the multitude to deal kindly with them, and permitted them to send to those that were their own hostages with Gessius to Dora, which is a city of Phoenicia, as often as they pleased; though I still found the inhabitants of Tiberias ready to take arms, and that on the occasion following: -

9. There were three factions in this city. The first was composed of men of worth and gravity; of these Julius Capellus was the head. Now he, as well as all his companions, Herod the son of Miarus, and Herod the son of Gamalus, and Compsus the son of Compsus; (for as to Compsus's brother Crispus, who had once been governor of the city under the great king [Agrippa] he was beyond Jordan in his own possessions;) all these persons before named gave their advice, that the city should then continue in their allegiance to the Romans

and to the king. But Pistus, who was guided by his son Justus, did not acquiesce in that resolution; otherwise he was himself naturally of a good and virtuous character. But the second faction was composed of the most ignoble persons, and was determined for war. But as for Justus, the son of Pistus, who was the head of the third faction, although he pretended to be doubtful about going to war, yet was he really desirous of innovation, as supposing that he should gain power to himself by the change of affairs. He therefore came into the midst of them, and endeavored to inform the multitude that "the city Tiberius had ever been a city of Galilee, and that in the days of Herod the tetrarch, who had built it, it had obtained the principal place, and that he had ordered that the city Sepphoris should be subordinate to the city Tiberias; that they had not lost this preeminence even under Agrippa the father, but had retained it until Felix was procurator of Judea. But he told them, that now they had been so unfortunate as to be made a present by Nero to Agrippa, junior; and that, upon Sepphoris's submission of itself to the Romans, that was become the capital city of Galilee, and that the royal library and the archives were now removed from them." When he had spoken these things, and a great many more, against king Agrippa, in order to provoke the people to a revolt, he added that "this was the time for them to take arms, and join with the Galileans as their confederates (whom they might command, and who would now willingly assist them, out of the hatred they bare to the people of Sepphoris; because they preserved their fidelity to the Romans), and to gather a great number of forces, in order to punish them." And as he said this, he exhorted the multitude, [to go to war;] for his abilities lay in making harangues to the people, and in being too hard in his speeches for such as opposed him, though they advised what was more to their advantage, and this by his craftiness and his fallacies, for he was not unskilful in the learning of the Greeks; and in dependence on that skill it was, that he undertook to write a history of these affairs, as aiming, by this way of haranguing, to disguise the truth. But as to this man, and how ill were his character and conduct of life, and how he and his brother were, in great measure, the authors of our destruction, I shall give the reader an account in the progress of my narration. So when Justus had, by his persuasions, prevailed with the citizens of Tiberias to take arms, nay, and had forced a great many so to do against their wills, he went out, and set the villages that belonged to Gadara and Hippos on fire; which villages were situated on the borders of Tiberias, and of the region of Scythopolis.

10. And this was the state Tiberias was now in. But as for Gischala, its affairs were thus: - When John, the son of Levi, saw some of the citizens much elevated upon their revolt from the Romans, he labored to restrain them, and

entreated them that they would keep their allegiance to them. But he could not gain his purpose, although he did his endeavors to the utmost; for the neighboring people of Gadara, Gabara, and Sogana, wth the Tyrians, got together a great army, and fell upon Gischala, and took Gischala by force, and set it on fire; and when they had entirely demolished it, they returned home. Upon which John was so enraged, that he armed all his men, and joined battle with the people forementioned; and rebuilt Gischala after a manner better than before, and fortified it with walls for its future security.

11. But Gamala persevered in its allegiance to the Romans, for the reason following: - Philip, the son of Jacimus, who was their governor under king Agrippa, had been unexpectedly preserved when the royal palace at Jerusalem had been besieged; but, as he fled away, had fallen into another danger, and that was, of being killed by Manahem, and the robbers that were with him; but certain Babylonians, who were of his kindred, and were then in Jerusalem, hindered the robbers from executing their design. So Philip staid there four days, and fled away on the fifth, having disguised himself with fictitious hair, that he might not be discovered; and when he was come to one of the villages to him belonging, but one that was situated at the borders of the citadel of Gamala, he sent to some of those that were under him, and commanded them to come to him. But God himself hindered that his intention, and this for his own advantage also; for had it not so happened, he had certainly perished. For a fever having seized upon him immediately, he wrote to Agrippa and Bernice, and gave them to one of his freed-men to carry them to Varus, who at this time was procurator of the kingdom, which the king and his sister had intrusted him withal, while they were gone to Berytus with an intention of meeting Gessius. When Varus had received these letters of Philip, and had learned that he was preserved, he was very uneasy at it, as supposing that he should appear useless to the king and his sister, now Philip was come. He therefore produced the carrier of the letters before the multitude, and accused him of forging the same; and said that he spake falsely when he related that Philip was at Jerusalem, fighting among the Jews against the Romans. So he slew him. And when this freed-man of Philip did not return again, Philip was doubtful what should be the occasion of his stay, and sent a second messenger with letters, that he might, upon his return, inform him what had befallen the other that had been sent before, and why he tarried so long. Varus accused this messenger also, when he came, of telling a falsehood, and slew him. For he was puffed up by the Syrians that were at Caesarea, and had great expectations; for they said that Agrippa would be slain by the Romans for the crimes which the Jews had committed, and that he should himself take the government, as derived from

their kings; for Varus was, by the confession of all, of the royal family, as being a descendant of Sohemus, who had enjoyed a tetrarchy about Libanus; for which reason it was that he was puffed up, and kept the letters to himself. He contrived, also, that the king should not meet with those writings, by guarding all the passes, lest any one should escape, and inform the king what had been done. He moreover slew many of the Jews, in order to gratify the Syrians of Cesarea. He had a mind also to join with the Trachonites in Batanea, and to take up arms and make an assault upon the Babylonian Jews that were at Ecbatana; for that was the name they went by. He therefore called to him twelve of the Jews of Cesarea, of the best character, and ordered them to go to Ecbatana, and inform their countrymen who dwelt there, That Varus hath heard that "you intend to march against the king; but, not believing that report, he hath sent us to persuade you to lay down your arms, and that this compliance will be a sign that he did well not to give credit to those that raised the report concerning you." He also enjoined them to send seventy of their principal men to make a defense for them as to the accusation laid against them. So when the twelve messengers came to their countrymen at Ecbatana, and found that they had no designs of innovation at all, they persuaded them to send the seventy men also; who, not at all suspecting what would come, sent them accordingly. So these seventy went down to Caesarea, together with the twelve ambassadors; where Varus met them with the king's forces, and slew them all, together with the [twelve] ambassadors, and made an expedition against the Jews of Ecbatana. But one there was of the seventy who escaped, and made haste to inform the Jews of their coming; upon which they took their arms, with their wives and children, and retired to the citadel at Gamala, leaving their own villages full of all sorts of good things, and having many ten thousands of cattle therein. When Philip was informed of these things, he also came to the citadel of Gamala; and when he was come, the multitude cried aloud, and desired him to resume the government, and to make an expedition against Varus, and the Syrians of Cesarea; for it was reported that they had slain the king. But Philip restrained their zeal, and put them in mind of the benefits the king had bestowed upon them; and told them how powerful the Romans were, and said it was not for their advantage to make war with them; and at length he prevailed with them. But now, when the king was acquainted with Varus's design, which was to cut off the Jews of Caesarea, being many ten thousands, with their wives and children, and all in one day, he called to him Equiculus Modius, and sent him to be Varus's successor, as we have elsewhere related. But still Philip kept possession of the citadel of Gamala, and of the country adjoining to it, which thereby continued in their allegiance to the Romans.

12. Now, as soon as I was come into Galilee, and had learned this state of things by the information of such as told me of them, I wrote to the sanhedrim at Jerusalem about them, and required their direction what I should do. Their direction was, that I should continue there, and that, if my fellow legates were willing, I should join with them in the care of Galilee. But those my fellow legates, having gotten great riches from those tithes which as priests were their dues, and were given to them, determined to return to their own country. Yet when I desired them to stay so long, that we might first settle the public affairs, they complied with me. So I removed, together with them, from the city of Sepphoris, and came to a certain village called Bethmaus, four furlongs distant from Tiberius; and thence I sent messengers to the senate of Tiberius, and desired that the principal men of the city would come to me: and when they were come, Justus himself being also with them, I told them that I was sent to them by the people of Jerusalem as a legate, together with these other priests, in order to persuade them to demolish that house which Herod the tetrarch had built there, and which had the figures of living creatures in it, although our laws have forbidden us to make any such figures; and I desired that they would give us leave so to do immediately. But for a good while Capellus and the principal men belonging to the city would not give us leave, but were at length entirely overcome by us, and were induced to be of our opinion. So Jesus the son of Sapphias, one of those whom we have already mentioned as the leader of a seditious tumult of mariners and poor people, prevented us, and took with him certain Galileans, and set the entire palace on fire, and thought he should get a great deal of money thereby, because he saw some of the roofs gilt with gold. They also plundered a great deal of the furniture, which was done without our approbation; for after we had discoursed with Capellus and the principal men of the city, we departed from Bethmaus, and went into the Upper Galilee. But Jesus and his party slew all the Greeks that were inhabitants of Tiberias, and as many others as were their enemies before the war began.

13. When I understood this state of things, I was greatly provoked, and went down to Tiberias, and took all the care I could of the royal furniture, to recover all that could be recovered from such as had plundered it. They consisted of candlesticks made of Corinthian brass, and of royal tables, and of a great quantity of uncoined silver; and I resolved to preserve whatsoever came to my hand for the king. So I sent for ten of the principal men of the senate, and for Capellus the son of Antyllus, and committed the furniture to them,

with this charge, That they should part with it to nobody else but to myself. From thence I and my fellow legates went to Gichala, to John, as desirous to know his intentions, and soon saw that he was for innovations, and had a mind to the principality; for he desired me to give him authority to carry off that corn which belonged to Caesar, and lay in the villages of Upper Galilee; and he pretended that he would expend what it came to in building the walls of his own city. But when I perceived what he endeavored at, and what he had in his mind, I said I would not permit him so to do; for that I thought either to keep it for the Romans or for myself, now I was intrusted with the public affairs there by the people of Jerusalem. But, when he was not able to prevail with me, he betook himself to my fellow legates; for they had no sagacity in providing for futurity, and were very ready to take bribes. So he corrupted them with money to decree, That all that corn which was within his province should be delivered to him; while I, who was but one, was outvoted by two, and held my tongue. Then did John introduce another cunning contrivance of his; for he said that those Jews who inhabited Cesarea Philippi, and were shut up by the order of the king's deputy there, had sent to him to desire him, that, since they had no oil that was pure for their use, he would provide a sufficient quantity of such oil for them, lest they should be forced to make use of oil that came from the Greeks, and thereby transgress their own laws. Now this was said by John, not out of his regard to religion, but out of his most flagrant desire of gain; for he knew that two sextaries were sold with them of Caesarea for one drachma, but that at Gischala fourscore sextaxies were sold for four sextaries. So he gave order that all the oil which was there should be carried away, as having my permission for so doing; which yet I did not grant him voluntarily, but only out of fear of the multitude, since, if I had forbidden him, I should have been stoned by them. When I had therefore permitted this to be done by John, he gained vast sums of money by this his knavery.

14. But when I had dismissed my fellow legates, and sent them back to Jerusalem, I took care to have arms provided, and the cities fortified. And when I had sent for the most hardy among the robbers, I saw that it was not in my power to take their arms from them; but I persuaded the multitude to allow them money as pay, and told them it was better for them to give them a little willingly, rather than to [be forced to] overlook them when they plundered their goods from them. And when I had obliged them to take an oath not to come into that country, unless they were invited to come, or else when they had not their pay given them, I dismissed them, and charged them neither to make an expedition against the Romans, nor against those their neighbors that lay round about them; for my first care was to keep Galilee in peace. So I was

willing to have the principal of the Galileans, in all seventy, as hostages for their fidelity, but still under the notion of friendship. Accordingly, I made them my friends and companions as I journeyed, and set them to judge causes; and with their approbation it was that I gave my sentences, while I endeavored not to mistake what justice required, and to keep my hands clear of all bribery in those determinations.

15. I was now about the thirtieth year of my age; in which time of life it is a hard thing for any one to escape the calumnies of the envious, although he restrain himself from fulfilling any unlawful desires, especially where a person is in great authority. Yet did I preserve every woman free from injuries; and as to what presents were offered me, I despised them, as not standing in need of them. Nor indeed would I take those tithes, which were due to me as a priest, from those that brought them. Yet do I confess, that I took part of the spoils of those Syrians which inhabited the cities that adjoined to us, when I had conquered them, and that I sent them to my kindred at Jerusalem; although, when I twice took Sepphoris by force, and Tiberias four times, and Gadara once, and when I had subdued and taken John, who often laid treacherous snares for me, I did not punish [with death] either him or any of the people forenamed, as the progress of this discourse will show. And on this account, I suppose, it was that God, who is never unacquainted with those that do as they ought to do, delivered me still out of the hands of these my enemies, and afterwards preserved me when I fell into those many dangers which I shall relate hereafter.

16. Now the multitude of the Galileans had that great kindness for me, and fidelity to me, that when their cities were taken by force, and their wives and children carried into slavery, they did not so deeply lament for their own calamities, as they were solicitous for my preservation. But when John saw this, he envied me, and wrote to me, desiring that I would give him leave to come down, and make use of the hot-baths of Tiberias for the recovery of the health of his body. Accordingly, I did not hinder him, as having no suspicion of any wicked designs of his; and I wrote to those to whom I had committed the administration of the affairs of Tiberius by name, that they should provide a lodging for John, and for such as should come with him, and should procure him what necessaries soever he should stand in need of. Now at this time my abode was in a village of Galilee, which is named Cans.

17. But when John was come to the city of Tiberias, he persuaded the men to revolt from their fidelity to me, and to adhere to him; and many of them gladly received that invitation of his, as ever fond of innovations, and by nature disposed to changes, and delighting in seditions; but they were chiefly Justus and his father Pistus, that were earnest for their revolt from me, and their

adherence to John. But I came upon them, and prevented them; for a messenger had come to me from Silas, whom I had made governor of Tiberias, as I have said already, and had told me of the inclinations of the people of Tiberias, and advised me to make haste thither; for that, if I made any delay, the city would come under another's jurisdiction. Upon the receipt of this letter of Silas, I took two hundred men along with me, and traveled all night, having sent before a messenger to let the people of Tiberias know that I was coming to them. When I came near to the city, which was early in the morning, the multitude came out to meet me; and John came with them, and saluted me, but in a most disturbed manner, as being afraid that my coming was to call him to an account for what I was now sensible he was doing. So he, in great haste, went to his lodging. But when I was in the open place of the city, having dismissed the guards I had about me, excepting one, and ten armed men that were with him, I attempted to make a speech to the multitude of the people of Tiberias: and, standing on a certain elevated place, I entreated them not to be so hasty in their revolt; for that such a change in their behavior would be to their reproach, and that they would then justly be suspected by those that should be their governors hereafter, as if they were not likely to be faithful to them neither.

18. But before I had spoken all I designed, I heard one of my own domestics bidding me come down, for that it was not a proper time to take care of retaining the good-will of the people of Tiberias, but to provide for my own safety, and escape my enemies there; for John had chosen the most trusty of those armed men that were about him out of those thousand that he had with him, and had given them orders when he sent them, to kill me, having learned that I was alone, excepting some of my domestics. So those that were sent came as they were ordered, and they had executed what they came about, had I not leaped down from the elevation I stood on, and with one of my guards, whose name was James, been carried [out of the crowd] upon the back of one Herod of Tiberias, and guided by him down to the lake, where I seized a ship, and got into it, and escaped my enemies unexpectedly, and came to Tarichese.

19. Now, as soon as the inhabitants of that city understood the perfidiousness of the people of Tiberias, they were greatly provoked at them. So they snatched up their arms, and desired me to be their leader against them; for they said they would avenge their commander's cause upon them. They also carried the report of what had been done to me to all the Galileans, and eagerly endeavored to irritate them against the people of Tiberias, and desired that vast numbers of them would get together, and come to them, that they might act in concert with their commander, what should be determined as fit to be done.

Accordingly, the Galileans came to me in great numbers, from all parts, with their weapons, and besought me to assault Tiberias, to take it by force, and to demolish it, till it lay even with the ground, and then to make slaves of its inhabitants, with their wives and children. Those that were Josephus's friends also, and had escaped out of Tiberias, gave him the same advice. But I did not comply with them, thinking it a terrible thing to begin a civil war among them; for I thought that this contention ought not to proceed further than words; nay, I told them that it was not for their own advantage to do what they would have me to do, while the Romans expected no other than that we should destroy one another by our mutual seditions. And by saying this, I put a stop to the anger of the Galileans.

20. But now John was afraid for himself, since his treachery had proved unsuccessful. So he took the armed men that were about him, and removed from Tiberias to Gischala, and wrote to me to apologize for himself concerning What had been done, as if it had been done without his approbation, and desired me to have no suspicion of him to his disadvantage. He also added oaths and certain horrible curses upon himself, and supposed he should be thereby believed in the points he wrote about to me.

21. But now another great number of the Galileans came together again with their weapons, as knowing the man, how wicked and how sadly perjured he was, and desired me to lead them against him and promised me that they would utterly both him and Gischala. Hereupon I professed that I was obliged to them for their readiness to serve me, and that I would more than requite their good-will to me. However, I entreated them to restrain themselves, and begged of them to give me leave to do what I intended, which was to put an end to these troubles without bloodshed; and when I had prevailed with the multitude of the Galileans to let me do so, I came to Sepphoris.

22. But the inhabitants of this city having determined to continue in their allegiance to the Romans, were afraid of my coming to them, and tried, by putting me upon another action, to divert me, that they might be freed from the terror they were in. Accordingly, they sent to Jesus, the captain of those robbers who were in the confines of Ptolemais, and promised to give him a great deal of money, if he would come with those forces he had with him, which were in number eight hundred, and fight with us. Accordingly, he complied with what they desired, upon the promises they had made him, and was desirous to fall upon us when we were unprepared for him, and knew nothing of his coming beforehand. So he sent to me, and desired that I would give him leave to come and salute me. When I had given him that leave, which I did without the least knowledge of his treacherous intentions beforehand, he

took his band of robbers, and made haste to come to me. Yet did not this his knavery succeed well at last; for as he was already nearly approaching, one of those with him deserted him, and came to me, and told me what he had undertaken to do. When I was informed of this, I went into the market-place, and pretended to know nothing of his treacherous purpose. I took with me many Galileans that were armed, as also some of those of Tiberias; and, when I had given orders that all the roads should be carefully guarded, I charged the keepers of the gates to give admittance to none but Jesus, when he came, with the principal of his men, and to exclude the rest; and in case they aimed to force themselves in, to use stripes [in order to repel them]. Accordingly, those that had received such a charge did as they were bidden, and Jesus came in with a few others; and when I had ordered him to throw down his arms immediately, and told him, that if he refused so to do, he was a dead man, he seeing armed men standing all round about him, was terrified, and complied; and as for those of his followers that were excluded, when they were informed that he was seized, they ran away. I then called Jesus to me by himself, and told him, that" I was not a stranger to that treacherous design he had against me, nor was I ignorant by whom he was sent for; that, however, I would forgive him what he had done already, if he would repent of it, and be faithful to me hereafter." And thus, upon his promise to do all that I desired, I let him go, and gave him leave to get those whom he had formerly had with him together again. But I threatened the inhabitants of Sepphoris, that, if they would not leave off their ungrateful treatment of me, I would punish them sufficiently.

23. At this time it was that two great men, who were under the jurisdiction of the king [Agrippa] came to me out of the region of Trachonius, bringing their horses and their arms, and carrying with them their money also; and when the Jews would force them to be circumcised, if they would stay among them, I would not permit them to have any force put upon them, but said to them, "Every one ought to worship God according to his own inclinations, and not to be constrained by force; and that these men, who had fled to us for protection, ought not to be so treated as to repent of their coming hither." And when I had pacified the multitude, I provided for the men that were come to us whatsoever it was they wanted, according to their usual way of living, and that in great plenty also.

24. Now king Agrippa sent an army to make themselves masters of the citadel of Gamala, and over it Equieulus Modius; but the forces that were sent were not allow to encompass the citadel quite round, but lay before it in the open places, and besieged it. But when Ebutius the decurion, who was intrusted with the government of the great plain, heard that I was at Simonias, a

village situated in the confines of Galilee, and was distant from him sixty furlongs, he took a hundred horsemen that were with him by night, and a certain number of footmen, about two hundred, and brought the inhabitants of the city Gibea along with him as auxiliaries, and marched in the night, and came to the village where I abode. Upon this I pitched my camp over against him, which had a great number of forces in it: but Ebutius tried to draw us down into the plain, as greatly depending upon his horsemen; but we would not come down; for when I was satisfied of the advantage that his horse would have if we came down into the plain, while we were all footmen, I resolved to join battle with the enemy where I was. Now Ebutius and his party made a courageous opposition for some time; but when he saw that his horse were useless to him in that place, he retired back to the city Gibea, having lost three of his men in the fight. So I followed him directy with two thousand armed men; and when I was at the city Besara, that lay in the confines of Ptolemais, but twenty furlongs from Gibea, where Ebutius abode, I placed my armed men on the outside of the village, and gave orders that they should guard the passes with great care, that the enemy might not disturb us until we should have carried off the corn, a great quantity of which lay there: it belonged to Bernice the queen, and had been gathered together out of the neighboring villages into Besara; so I loaded my camels and asses, a great number of which I had brought along with me, and sent the corn into Galilee. When I had done this, I offered Ebutius battle; but when he would not accept of the offer, for he was terrified at our readiness and courage, I altered my route, and marched towards Neopolitanus, because I had heard that the country about Tiberias was laid waste by him. This Neopolitanus was captain of a troop of horse, and had the custody of Scythopolis intrusted to his care by the enemy; and when I had hindered him from doing any further mischief to Tiberias, I set myself to make provision for the affairs of Galilee.

25. But when John, the son of Levi, who, as we before told you, abode at Gischala, was informed how all things had succeeded to my mind, and that I was much in favor with those that were under me, as also that the enemy were greatly afraid of me, he was not pleased with it, as thinking my prosperity tended to his ruin. So he took up a bitter envy and enmity against me; and hoping, that if he could inflame those that were under me to hate me,. he should put an end to the prosperity I was in, he tried to persuade the inhabitants of Tiberias and of Sepphoris, (and for those of Gabara he supposed they would be also of the same mind with the others,) which were the greatest cities of Galilee, to revolt from their subjection to me, and to be of his party; and told them that he would command them better than I did. As for the people of

Sepphoris, who belonged to neither of us, because they had chosen to be in subjection to the Romans, they did not comply with his proposal; and for those of Tiberias, they did not indeed so far comply as to make a revolt from under me, but they agreed to be his friends, while the inhabitants of Gabara did go over to John; and it was Simon that persuaded them so to do, one who was both the principal man in the city, and a particular friend and companion of John. It is true, these did not openly own the making a revolt, because they were in great fear of the Galileans, and had frequent experience of the good-will they bore to me; yet did they privately watch for a proper opportunity to lay snares for me; and indeed I thereby came into the greatest danger, on the occasion following.

26. There were some bold young men of the village of Dabaritta, who observed that the wife of Ptolemy, the king's procurator, was to make a progress over the great plain with a mighty attendance, and with some horsemen that followed as a guard to them, and this out of a country that was subject to the king and queen, into the jurisdiction of the Romans; and fell upon them on a sudden, and obliged the wife of Ptolemy to fly away, and plundered all the carriages. They also came to me to Tarichese, with four mules' loading of garments, and other furniture; and the weight of the silver they brought was not small, and there were five hundred pieces of gold also. Now I had a mind to preserve these spoils for Ptolemy, who was my countryman; and it is prohibited by our laws even to spoil our enemies; so I said to those that brought these spoils, that they ought to be kept, in order to rebuild the walls of Jerusalem with them when they came to be sold. But the young men took it very ill that they did not receive a part of those spoils for themselves, as they expected to have done; so they went among the villages in the neighborhood of Tiberias, and told the people that I was going to betray their country to the Romans, and that I used deceitful language to them, when I said, that what had been thus gotten by rapine should be kept for the rebuilding of the walls of the city of Jerusalem; although I had resolved to restore these spoils again to their former owner. And indeed they were herein not mistaken as to my intentions; for when I had gotten clear of them, I sent for two of the principal men, Dassion, and Janneus the son of Levi, persons that were among the chief friends of the king, and commanded them to take the furniture that had been plundered, and to send it to him; and I threatened that I would order them to be put to death by way of punishment, if they discovered this my command to any other person.

27. Now, when all Galilee was filled with this rumor, that their country was about to be betrayed by me to the Romans, and when all men were exasperated

against me, and ready to bring me to punishment, the inhabitants of Tarichee did also themselves suppose that what the young men said was true, and persuaded my guards and armed men to leave me when I was asleep, and to come presently to the hippodrome, in order there to take counsel against me their commander. And when they had prevailed with them, and they were gotten together, they found there a great company assembled already, who all joined in one clamor, to bring the man who was so wicked to them as to betray them, to his due punishment; and it was Jesus, the son of Sapphias, who principally set them on. He was ruler in Tiberias, a wicked man, and naturally disposed to make disturbances in matters of consequence; a seditious person he was indeed, and an innovator beyond every body else. He then took the laws of Moses into his hands, and came into the midst of the people, and said," O my fellow citizens! if you are not disposed to hate Josephus on your own account, have regard, however, to these laws of your country, which your commander-in-chief is going to betray; hate him therefore on both these accounts, and bring the man who hath acted thus insolently, to his deserved punishment."

28. When he had said this, and the multitude had openly applauded him for what he had said, he took some of the armed men, and made haste away to the house in which I lodged, as if he would kill me immediately, while I was wholly insensible of all till this disturbance happened; and by reason of the pains I had been taking, was fallen fast asleep. But Simon, who was intrusted with the care of my body, and was the only person that stayed with me, and saw the violent incursion the citizens made upon me, awaked me, and told me of the danger I was in, and desired me to let him kill me, that I might die bravely and like a general, before my enemies came in, and forced me [to kill myself], or killed me themselves. Thus did he discourse to me; but I committed the care of my life to God, and made haste to go out to the multitude. Accordingly, I put on a black garment, and hung my sword at my neck, and went by such a different way to the hippodrome, wherein I thought none of my adversaries would meet me; so I appeared among them on the sudden, and fell down flat on the earth, and bedewed the ground with my tears: then I seemed to them all an object of compassion. And when I perceived the change that was made in the multitude, I tried to divide their opinions before the armed men should return from my house; so I granted them that I had been as wicked as they supposed me to be; but still I entreated them to let me first inform them for what use I had kept that money which arose from the plunder, and, that they might then kill me if they pleased: and upon the multitude's ordering me to speak, the armed men came upon me, and when they saw me, they ran to kill me; but when the multitude bade them hold their

hands, they complied, and expected that as soon as I should own to them that I kept the money for the king, it would be looked on as a confession of my treason, and they should then be allowed to kill me.

29. When, therefore, silence was made by the whole multitude, I spake thus to them: "O my countrymen! I refuse not to die, if justice so require. However, I am desirous to tell you the truth of this matter before I die; for as I know that this city of yours [Tarichee] was a city of great hospitality, and filled with abundance of such men as have left their own countries, and are come hither to be partakers of your fortune, whatever it be, I had a mind to build walls about it, out of this money, for which you are so angry with me, while yet it was to be expended in building your own walls." Upon my saying this, the people of Taricheae and the strangers cried out, that" they gave me thanks, and desired me to be of good courage," although the Galileans and the people of Tiberias continued in their wrath against me, insomuch that there arose a tumult among them, while some threatened to kill me, and some bade me not to regard them; but when I promised them that I would build them walls at Tiberias, and at other cities that wanted them, they gave credit to what I promised, and returned every one to his own home. So I escaped the foremen-tioned danger, beyond all my hopes, and returned to my own house, accom-panied with my friends, and twenty armed men also.

30. However, these robbers and other authors of this tumult, who were afraid, on their own account, lest I should punish them for what they had done, took six hundred armed men, and came to the house where I abode, in order to set it on fire. When this their insult was told me, I thought it indecent for me to run away, and I resolved to expose myself to danger, and to act with some boldness; so I gave order to shut the doors, and went up into an upper room, and desired that they would send in some of their men to receive the money [from the spoils] for I told them they would then have no occasion to be angry with me; and when they had sent in one of the boldest of them all, I had him whipped severely, and I commanded that one of his hands should be cut off, and hung about his neck; and in this case was he put out to those that sent him. At which procedure of mine they were greatly affrighted, and in no small consternation, and were afraid that they should themselves be served in like manner, if they staid there; for they supposed that I had in the house more armed men than they had themselves; so they ran away immediately, while I, by the use of this stratagem, escaped this their second treacherous design against me.

31. But there were still some that irritated the multitude against me, and said that those great men that belonged to the king ought not to be suffered to

live, if they would not change their religion to the religion of those to whom they fled for safety: they spake reproachfully of them also, and said that they were wizards, and such as called in the Romans upon them. So the multitude was soon deluded by such plausible pretenses as were agreeable to their own inclinations, and were prevailed on by them. But when I was informed of this, I instructed the multitude again, that those who fled to them for refuge ought not to be persecuted: I also laughed at the allegation about witchcraft, and told them that the Romans would not maintain so many ten thousand soldiers, if they could overcome their enemies by wizards. Upon my saying this, the people assented for a while; but they returned again afterwards, as irritated by some ill people against the great men; nay, they once made an assault upon the house in which they dwelt at Tarichess, in order to kill them; which, when I was informed of, I was afraid lest so horrid a crime should take effect, and nobody else would make that city their refuge any more. I therefore came myself, and some others with me, to the house where these great men lived, and locked the doors, and had a trench drawn from their house leading to the lake, and sent for a ship, and embarked therein with them, and sailed to the confines of Hippos: I also paid them the value of their horses; nor in such a flight could I have their horses brought to them. I then dismissed them, and begged of them earnestly that they would courageously bear I this distress which befell them. I was also myself I greatly displeased that I was compelled to expose those that had fled to me to go again into an enemy's country; yet did I think it more eligible that they should perish among the Romans, if it should so happen, than in the country that was under my jurisdiction. However, they escaped at length, and king Agrippa forgave them their offenses. And this was the conclusion of what concerned these men.

32. But as for the inhabitants of the city of Tiberias, they wrote to the king, and desired him to send them forces sufficient to be a guard to their country; for that they were desirous to come over to him: this was what they wrote to him. But when I came to them, they desired me to build their walls, as I had promised them to do; for they had heard that the walls of Tarichess were already built. I agreed to their proposal accordingly; and when I had made preparation for the entire building, I gave order to the architects to go to work; but on the third day, when I was gone to Tarichess, which was thirty furlongs distant from Tiberias, it so fell out, that some Roman horsemen were discovered on their march, not far from the city, which made it to be supposed that the forces were come from the king; upon which they shouted, and lifted up their voices in commendations of the king, and in reproaches against me. Hereupon one came running to me, and told me what their dispositions were,

and that they had resolved to revolt from me: upon hearing which news I was very much alarmed; for I had already sent away my armed men from Tarichess, to their own homes, because the next day was our sabbath; for I would not have the people of Tarichess disturbed [on that day] by a multitude of soldiers; and indeed, whenever I sojourned at that city, I never took any particular care for a guard about my own body, because I had had frequent instances of the fidelity its inhabitants bore to me. I had now about me no more than seven armed men, besides some friends, and was doubtful what to do; for to send to recall my own forces I did not think proper, because the present day was almost over; and had those forces been with me, I could not take up arms on the next day, because our laws forbade us so to do, even though our necessity should be very great; and if I should permit the people of Tarichess, and the strangers with them, to guard the city, I saw that they would not be sufficient for that purpose, and I perceived that I should be obliged to delay my assistance a great while; for I thought with myself that the forces that came from the king would prevent me, and that I should be driven out of the city. I considered, therefore, how to get clear of these forces by a stratagem; so I immediately placed those my friends of Tarichee, on whom I could best confide, at the gates, to watch those very carefully who went out at those gates: I also called to me the heads of families, and bade every one of them to seize upon a ship to go on board it, and to take a master with them, and follow him to the city of Tiberias. I also myself went on board one of those ships, with my friends, and the seven armed men already mentioned, and sailed for Tiberias.

33. But now, when the people of Tiberias perceived that there were no forces come from the king, and yet saw the whole lake full of ships, they were in fear what would become of their city, and were greatly terrified, as supposing that the ships were full of men on board; so they then changed their minds, and threw down their weapons, and met me with their wives and children, and made acclamations to me with great commendations; for they imagined that I did not know their former inclinations [to have been against me]; so they persuaded me to spare the city. But when I was come near enough, I gave order to the masters of the ships to cast anchor a good way off the land, that the people of Tiberias might not perceive that the ships had no men on board; but I went nearer to the people in one of the ships, and rebuked them for their folly, ,and that they were so fickle as, without any just occasion in the world, to revolt from their fidelity to me. However, assured them that I would entirely forgive them for the time to come, if they would send ten of the ringleaders of the multitude to me; and when they complied readily with this proposal,

and sent me the men forementioned, I put them on board a ship, and sent them away to Tarichese; and ordered them to be kept in prison.

34. And by this stratagem it was that I gradually got all the senate of Tiberias into my power, and sent them to the city forementioned, with many of the principal men among the populace, and those not fewer in number than the other. But when the multitude saw into what great miseries they had brought themselves, they desired me to punish the author of this sedition: his name was Clitus, a young man, bold and rash in his undertakings. Now, since I thought it not agreeable to piety to put one of my own people to death, and yet found it necessary to punish him, I ordered Levi, one of my own guards, to go to him, and cut off one of Clitus's hands; but as he that was ordered to do this, was afraid to go out of the ship alone, among 'so great a multitude, I was not willing that the timorousness of the soldier should appear to the people of Tiberias. So I called to Clitus himself and said to him," Since thou deservest to lose both thine hands for thy ingratitude to me, be thou thine own executioner, lest, if thou refusest so to be, thou undergo a worse punishment." And when he earnestly begged of me to spare him one of his hands, it was with difficulty that I granted it. So, in order to prevent the loss of both his hands, he willingly took his sword, and cut off his own left hand; and this put an end to the sedition.

35. Now the men of Tiberias, after I was gone to Taricheae, perceived what stratagem I had used against them, and they admired how I had put an end to their foolish sedition, without shedding of blood. But now, when I had sent for some of those multitudes of the people of Tiberias out of prison, among whom were Justus and his father Pistus, I made them to sup with me; and during our supper time I said to them, that I knew the power of the Romans was superior to all others, but did not say so [publicly] because of the robbers. So I advised them to do as I did, and to wait for a proper opportunity, and not to be uneasy at my being their commander; for that they could not expect to have another who would use the like moderation that I had done. I also put Justus in mind how the Galileans had cut off his brother's hands before ever I came to Jerusalem, upon an accusation laid against him, as if he had been a rogue, and had forged some letters; as also how the people of Gamala, in a sedition they raised against the Babylonians, after the departure of Philip, slew Chares, who was a kinsman of Philip, and withal how they had wisely punished Jesus, his brother Justuses sister's husband [with death]. When I had said this to them during supper time, I in the morning ordered Justus, and all the rest that were in prison, to be loosed out of it, and sent away.

36. But before this, it happened that Philip, the son of Jacimus, went out of the citadel of Gamala upon the following occasion: When Philip had been informed that Varus was put out of his government by king Agrippa, and that Equieulus Modius, a man that was of old his friend and companion, was come to succeed him, he wrote to him, and related what turns of fortune he had had, and desired him to forward the letters he sent to the king and queen. Now, when Modius had received these letters, he was exceedingly glad, and sent the letters to the king and queen, who were then about Berytus. But when king Agrippa knew that the story about Philip was false, (for it had been given out, that the Jews had begun a war with the Romans, and that this Philip had been their commander in that war,) he sent some horsemen to conduct Philip to him; and when he was come, he saluted him very obligingly, and showed him to the Roman commanders, and told them that this was the man of whom the report had gone about as if he had revolted from the Romans. He also bid him to take some horsemen with him, and to go quickly to the citadel of Gamala, and to bring out thence all his domestics, and to restore the Babylonians to Batanea again. He also gave it him in charge to take all possible care that none of his subjects should be guilty of making any innovation. Accordingly, upon these directions from the king, he made haste to do what he was commanded.

37. Now there was one Joseph, the son of a female physician, who excited a great many young men to join with him. He also insolently addressed himself to the principal persons at Gamala, and persuaded them to revolt from the king; and take up arms, and gave them hopes that they should, by his means, recover their liberty. And some they forced into the service, and those that would not acquiesce in what they had resolved on, they slew. They also slew Chares, and with him Jesus, one of his kinsmen, and a brother of Justus of Tiberias, as we have already said. Those of Gamala also wrote to me, desiring me to send them an armed force, and workmen to raise up the walls of their city; nor did I reject either of their requests. The region of Gaulanitis did also revolt from the king, as far as the village Solyma. I also built a wall about Seleucia and Soganni, which are villages naturally of ver great strength. Moreover, I, in like manner, walled several villages of Upper Galilee, though they were very rocky of themselves. Their names are Jamnia, and Meroth, and Achabare. I also fortified, in the Lower Galilee, the cities Tarichee, Tiberias, Sepphoris, and the villages, the cave of Arbela, Bersobe, Selamin, Jotapata, Capharecho, and Sigo, and Japha, and Mount Tabor. I also laid up a great quantity of corn in these places, and arms withal, that might be for their security afterward.

38. But the hatred that John, the son of Levi, bore to me, grew now more violent, while he could not bear my prosperity with patience. So he proposed to himself, by all means possible, to make away with me; and built the walls of Gischala, which was the place of his nativity. He then sent his brother Simon, and Jonathan, the son of Sisenna, and about a hundred armed men, to Jerusalem, to Simon, the son of Gamaliel, in order to persuade him to induce the commonalty of Jerusalem to take from me the government over the Galileans, and to give their suffrages for conferring that authority upon him. This Simon was of the city of Jerusalem, and of a very noble family of the sect of the Pharisees, which are supposed to excel others in the accurate knowledge of the laws of their country. He was a man of great wisdom and reason, and capable of restoring public affairs by his prudence, when they were in an ill posture. He was also an old friend and companion of John; but at that time he had a difference with me. When therefore he had received such an exhortation, he persuaded the high priests, Ananus, and Jesus the son of Gamala, and some others of the same seditious faction, to cut me down, now I was growing so great, and not to overlook me while I was aggrandizing myself to the height of glory; and he said that it would be for the advantage of the Galileans, if I were deprived of my government there. Ananus also, and his friends, desired them to make no delay about the matter, lest I should get the knowledge of what was doing too soon, and should come and make an assault upon the city with a great army. This was the counsel of Simon; but Artanus the high priest demonstrated to them that this was not an easy thing to be done, because many of the high priests and of the rulers of the people bore witness that I had acted like an excellent general, and that it was the work of ill men to accuse one against whom they had nothing to say.

39. When Simon heard Ananus say this, he desired that the messengers would conceal the thing, and not let it come among many; for that he would take care to have Josephus removed out of Galilee very quickly. So he called for John's brother, [Simon,] and charged him that they should send presents to Ananus and his friends; for, as he said, they might probably by that means persuade them to change their minds. And indeed Simon did at length thus compass what he aimed at; for Artanus, and those with him, being corrupted by bribes, agreed to expel me out of Galilee, without making the rest of the citizens acquainted with what they were doing. Accordingly, they resolved to send men of distinction as to their families, and of distinction as to their learning also. Two of these were of the populace, Jonathan and Ananias, by sect Pharisees; while the third, Jozar, was of the stock of the priests, and a Pharisee also; and Simon, the last of them, was of the youngest of the high

priests. These had it given them in charge, that, when they were come to the multitude of the Galileans, they should ask them, what was the reason of their love to me? and if they said that it was because I was born at Jerusalem, that they should reply, that they four were all born at the same place; and if they should say, it was because I was well versed in their law, they should reply, that neither were they unacquainted with the practices of their country; but if, besides these, they should say, they loved me because I was a priest, they should reply, that two of these were priests also.

40. Now, when they had given Jonathan and his companions these instructions, they gave them forty thousand [drachmae] out of the public money: but when they heard that there was a certain Galilean that then sojourned at Jerusalem, whose name was Jesus, who had about him a band of six hundred armed men, they sent for him, and gave him three months pay, and gave him orders to follow Jonathan and his companions, and be obedient to them. They also gave money to three hundred men that were citizens of Jerusalem, to maintain them all, and ordered them also to follow the ambassadors; and when they had complied, and were gotten ready for the march, Jonathan and his companions went out with them, having along with them John's brother and a hundred armed men. The charge that was given them by those that sent them was this: That if I would voluntarily lay down my arms, they should send me alive to the city of Jerusalem; but that, in case I opposed them, they should kill me, and fear nothing; for that it was their command for them so to do. They also wrote to John to make all ready for fighting me, and gave orders to the inhabitants of Sepphoris, and Gabara, and Tiberins, to send auxiliaries to John.

41. Now, as my father wrote me an account of this, (for Jesus the son of Gamala, who was present in that council, a friend and companion of mine, told him of it,) I was very much troubled, as discovering thereby that my fellow citizens proved so ungrateful to me, as, out of envy, to give order that I should be slain: my father earnestly pressed me also in his letter to come to him, for that he longed to see his son before he died. I informed my friends of these things, and that in three days' time I should leave the country, and go home. Upon hearing this, they were all very sorry, and desired me, with tears in their eyes, not to leave them to be destroyed; for so they thought they should be, if I were deprived of the command over them: but as I did not grant their request, but was taking care of my own safety, the Galileans, out of their dread of the consequence of my departure, that they should then be at the mercy of the robbers, sent messengers over all Galilee to inform them of my resolution to leave them. Whereupon, as soon as they heard it, they got togeth-

er in great numbers, from all parts, with their wives and children; and this they did, as it appeared to me, not more out of their affection to me, than out of their fear on their own account; for while I staid with them, they supposed that they should suffer no harm. So they all came into the great plain, wherein I lived, the name of which was Asochis.

42. But wonderful it was what a dream I saw that very night; for when I had betaken myself to my bed, as grieved and disturbed at the news that had been written to me, it seemed to me, that a certain person stood by me, and said, "O Josephus! leave off to afflict thy soul, and put away all fear; for what now grieves thee will render thee very considerable, and in all respects most happy; for thou shalt get over not only these difficulties, but many others, with great success. However, be not cast down, but remember that thou art to fight with the Romans." When I had seen this dream, I got up with an intention of going down to the plain. Now, when the whole multitude of the Galileans, among whom were the women and children, saw me, they threw themselves down upon their faces, and, with tears in their eyes, besought me not to leave them exposed to their enemies, nor to go away and permit their country to be injured by them. But when I did not comply, with their entreaties, they compelled me to take an oath, that I would stay with them: they also cast abundance of reproaches upon the people of Jerusalem, that they would not let their country enjoy peace.

43. When I heard this, and saw what sorrow the people were in, I was moved with compassion to them, and thought it became me to undergo the most manifest hazards for the sake of so great a multitude; so I let them know I would stay with them. And when I had given order that five thousand off them should come to me armed, and with provisions for their maintenance, I sent the rest away to their own homes; and when those five thousand were come, I took them, together with three thousand of the soldiers that were with me before, and eighty horsemen, and marched to thevillage of Chabolo, situated in the confines of Ptolimias, and there kept my forces together, pretending to get ready to fight with Placidus, who was come with two cohorts of footmen, and one troop of horsemen, and was sent thither by Cestius Gallus to burn those villages of Galilee that were near Ptolemais. Upon whose casting up a bank before the city Ptolemais, I also pitched my camp at about the distance of sixty furlongs from that village. And now we frequently brought out our forces as if we would fight, but proceeded no further than skirmishes at a distance; for when Placidus perceived that I was earnest to come to a battle, he was afraid, and avoided it. Yet did he not remove from the neighborhood of Ptolemais.

44. About this time it was that Jonathan and his fellow legates came. They were sent, as we have said already, by Simon, and Ananus the high priest. And Jonathan contrived how he might catch me by treachery; for he durst not make any attempt upon me openly. So he wrote me the following epistle: "Jonathan and those that are with him, and are sent by the people of Jerusalem, to Josephus, send greeting. We are sent by the principal men of Jerusalem, who have heard that John of Gischala hath laid many snares for thee, to rebuke him, and to exhort him to be subject to thee hereafter. We are also desirous to consult with thee about our common concerns, and what is fit to be done. We therefore desire thee to come to us quickly, and to bring only a few men with thee; for this village will not contain a great number of soldiers." Thus it was that they wrote, as expecting one of these two things; either that I should come without armed men, and then they should have me wholly in their power; or, if I came with a great number, they should judge me to be a public enemy. Now it was a horseman who brought the letter, a man at other times bold, and one that had served in the army under the king. It was the second hour of the night that he came, when I was feasting with my friends, and the principal of the Galileans. This man, upon my servant's telling me that a certain horseman of the Jewish nation was come, was called in at my command, but did not so much as salute me at all, but held out a letter, and said, "This letter is sent thee by those that are come from Jerusalem; do thou write an answer to it quickly; for I am obliged to return to them very soon. Now my guests could not but wonder at the boldness of the soldier. But I desired him to sit down and sup with us; but when he refused so to do, I held the letter in my hands as I received it, and fell a talking with my guests about other matters. But a few hours afterwards, I got up, and when I had dismissed the rest to go to their beds, I bid only four of my intimate friends to stay, and ordered my servant to get some wine ready. I also opened the letter so, that nobody could perceive it; and understanding thereby presently the purport· of the writing, I sealed it up again, and appeared as if I had not yet read it, but only held it in my hands. I ordered twenty drachmae should be given the soldier for the charges of his journey; and when he took the money, and said that he thanked me for it, I perceived that he loved money, and that he was to be caught chiefly by that means; and I said to him," If thou wilt but drink with us, thou shalt have a drachma for every glass thou drinkest." So he gladly embraced this proposal, and drank a great deal of wine, in order to get the more money, and was so drunk, that at last he could not keep the secrets he was intrusted with, but discovered them without my putting questions to him, viz. That a treacherous design was contrived against me, and that I was doomed to die by those

that sent him. When I heard this, I wrote back this answer: "Josephus to Jonathan, and those that are with him, sendeth greeting. Upon the information that you are come in health into Galilee, I rejoice, and this especially because I can now resign the care of public affairs here into your hands, and return into my native country, which is what I have desired to do a great while; and I confess I ought not only to come to you as far as Xaloth, but farther, and this without your commands. But I desire you to excuse me, because I cannot do it now, since I watch the motions of Placidus, who hath a mind to go up into Galilee; and this I do here at Chabolo. Do you therefore, on the receipt of this epistle, come hither to me. Fare you well."

45. When I had written thus, and given the letter to be carried by the soldier, I sent along with him thirty of the Galileans of the best characters, and gave them instructions to salute those ambassadors, but to say nothing else to them. I also gave orders to as many of those armed men, whom I esteemed most faithful to me, to go along with the others, every one with him whom he was to guard, lest some conversation might pass between those whom I sent and those who were with Jonathan. So those men went [to Jonathan]. But when Jonathan and his partners had failed in this their first attempt, they sent me another letter, the contents whereof were as follows: "Jonathan, and those with him, to Josephus, send greeting. We require thee to come to us to the village Gabaroth, on the third day, without any armed men, that we may hear what thou hast to lay to the charge of John [of Gischala]." When they had written this letter, they saluted the Galileans whom I sent, and came to Japha, which was the largest village of all Galilee, and encompassed with very strong walls, and had a great number of inhabitants in it. There the multitude of men, with their wives and children, met them, and exclaimed loudly against them; and desired them to be gone, and not to envy them the advantage of an excellent commander. With these clamors Jonathan and his partners were greatly provoked, although they durst not show their anger openly; so they made them no answer, but went to other villages. But still the same clamors met them from all the people, who said, "Nobody should persuade them to have any other commander besides Josephus." So Jonathan and his partners went away from them without success, and came to Sepphoris, the greatest city of all Galilee. Now the men of that city, who inclined to the Romans in their sentiments, met them indeed, but neither praised nor reproached me and when they were gone down from Sepphoris to Asochis, the people of that place made a clamor against them, as those of Japha had done; whereupon they were able to contain themselves no longer, but ordered the armed men that were with them to beat those that made the clamor with their clubs. And when they

came to Gabara, John met them with three thousand armed men; but, as I understood by their letter that they had resolved to fight against me, I arose from Chabolo, with three thousand armed men also; but left in my camp one of my fastest friends, and came to Jotapata, as desirous to be near them, the distance being no more than forty furlongs. Whence I wrote thus to them: "If you are very desirous that I should come to you, you know there are two hundred and forty cities and villages in Galilee; I will come to any of them which you please, excepting Gaburn and Gischala; the one of which is John's native city, and the other in confederacy and friendship with him."

46. When Jonathan and his partners had received this letter, they wrote me no more answers, but called a council of their friends together; and taking John into their consultation, they took counsel together by what means they might attack me. John's opinion was, that they should write to all the cities and villages that were in Galilee; for that there must be certainly one or two persons in every one of them that were at variance with me, and that they should be invited to come to oppose me as an enemy. He would also have them send this resolution of theirs to the city of Jerusalem, that its citizens, upon the knowledge of my being adjudged to be an enemy by the Galileans, might themselves I also confirm that determination. He said also, that when this was done, even those Galileans who were well affected to me, would desert me out of fear. When John had given them this counsel, what he had said was very agreeable to the rest of them. I was also made acquainted with these affairs about the third hour of the night, by the means of one Saccheus, who had belonged to them, but now deserted them and came over to me, and told me what they were about; so I perceived that no time was to be lost. Accordingly, I gave command to Jacob, an armed man of my guard, whom I esteemed faithful to me, to take two hundred men, and to guard the passages that led from Gahara to Galilee, and to seize upon the passengers, and send them to me, especially such as were caught with letters about them: I also sent Jeremias himself, one of my friends, with six hundred armed men, to the borders of Galilee, in order to watch the roads that led from this country to the city Jerusalem, and gave him charge to lay hold of such as traveled with letters about them, to keep the men in bonds upon the place, but to send me the letters.

47. When I had laid these commands upon them, I gave them orders, and bid them take their arms and bring three days' provision with them, and be with me the next day. I also parted those that were about me into four parts, and ordained those of them that were most faithful to me to be a guard to my body. I also set over them centurions, and commanded them to take care that

not a soldier which they did not know should mingle himself among them. Now, on the fifth day following, when I was at Gabaroth, I found the entire plain that was before the village full of armed men, who were come out of Galilee to assist me: many others of the multitude, also, out of the village, ran along with me. But as soon as I had taken my place, and began to speak to them, they all made an acclamation, and called me the benefactor and savior of the country. And when I had made them my acknowledgments, and thanked them [for their affection to me], I also advised them to fight with nobody, nor to spoil the country; but to pitch their tents in the plain, and be content with their sustenance they had brought with them; for I told them that I had a mind to compose these troubles without shedding any blood. Now it came to pass, that on the very same day those who were sent by John with letters, fell among the guards whom I had appointed to watch the roads; so the men were themselves kept upon the place, as my orders were, but I got the letters, which were full of reproaches and lies; and I intended to fall upon these men, without saying a word of these matters to any body.

48. Now, as soon as Jonathan and his companions heard of my coming, they took all their own friends, and John with them, and retired to the house of Jesus, which indeed was a large castle, and no way unlike a citadel; so they privately laid a band of armed men therein, and shut all the other doors but one, which they kept open, and they expected that I should come out of the road to them, to salute them. And indeed they had given orders to the armed men, that when I came they should let nobody besides me come in, but should exclude others; as supposing that, by this means, they should easily get me under their power: but they were deceived in their expectation; for I perceived what snares they had laid for me. Now, as soon as I was got off my journey, I took up my lodgings over against them, and pretended to be asleep; so Jonathan and his party, thinking that I was really asleep and at rest, made haste to go down into the plain, to persuade the people that I was an ill governor. But the matter proved otherwise; for, upon their appearance, there was a cry made by the Galileans immediately, declaring their good opinion of me as their governor; and they made a clamor against Jonathan and his partners for coming to them when they had suffered no harm, and as though they would overturn their happy settlement; and desired them by all means to go back again, for that they would never be persuaded to have any other to rule over them but myself. When I heard of this, I did not fear to go down into the midst of them; I went, therefore, myself down presently to hear what Jonathan and his companions said. As soon as I appeared, there was immediately an acclamation made to me by the whole multitude, and a cry in my commenda-

tion by them, who confessed their thanks was owing to me for my good government of them.

49. When Jonathan and his companions heard this, they were in fear of their own lives, and in danger lest they should be assaulted by the Galileans on nay account; so they contrived how they might run away. But as they were not able to get off, for I desired them to stay, they looked down with concern at my words to them. I ordered, therefore, the multitude to restrain entirely their acclamations, and placed the most faithful of my armed men upon the avenues, to be a guard to us, lest John should unexpected fall upon us; and I encouraged the Galileans to take their weapons, lest they should be disturbed at their enemies, if any sudden insult should be made upon them. And then, in the first place, I put Jonathan and his partners in mind of their [former] letter, and after what manner they had written to me, and declared they were sent by the common consent to the people of Jerusalem, to make up the differences I had with John, and how they had desired me to come to them; and as I spake thus, I publicly showed that letter they had written, till they could not at all deny what they had done, the letter itself convicting them. I then said, "O Jonathan! and you that are sent with him as his colleagues, if I were to be judged as to my behavior, compared with that of John's, and had brought no more than two or three witnesses, good men and true, it is plain you had been forced, upon the examination of their characters beforehand, to discharge the accusations: that therefore you may be informed that I have acted well in the affairs of Galilee, I think three witnesses too few to be brought by a man that hath done as he ought to do; so I gave you all these for witnesses. Inquire of them how I have lived, and whether I have not behaved myself with all decency, and after a virtuous manner, among them. And I further conjure you, O Galileans! to hide no part of the truth, but to speak before these men as before judges, whether I have in any thing acted otherwise than well."

50. While I was thus speaking, the united voices of all the people joined together, and called me their benefactor and savior, and attested to my former behavior, and exhorted me to continue so to do hereafter; and they all said, upon their oaths, that their wives had been preserved free from injuries, and that no one had ever been aggrieved by me. After this, I read to the Galileans two of those epistles which had been sent by Jonathan and his colleagues, and which those whom I had appointed to guard the road had taken, and sent to me. These were full of reproaches, and of lies, as if I had acted more like a tyrant than a governor against them, with many other things besides therein contained, which were no better indeed than impudent falsities. I also informed the multitude how I came by these letters, and that those who carried

them delivered them up voluntarily; for I was not willing that my enemies should know any thing of the guards I had set, lest they should be afraid, and leave off writing hereafter.

51. When the multitude heard these things, they were greatly provoked at Jonathan, and his colleagues that were with him, and were going to attack them, and kill them; and this they had certainly done, unless I had restrained the anger of the Galileans, and said, that" I forgave Jonathan and his colleagues what was past, if they would repent, and go to their own country, and tell those who sent them the truth, as to my conduct." When I had said this, I let them go, although I knew they would do nothing of what they had promised. But the multitude were very much enraged against them, and entreated me to give them leave to punish them for their insolence; yet did I try all methods to persuade them to spare the men; for I knew that every instance of sedition was pernicious to the public welfare. But the multitude was too angry with them to be dissuaded, and all of them went immediately to the house in which Jonathan and his colleagues abode. However, when I perceived that their rage could not be restrained, I got on horseback, and ordered the multitude to follow me to the village Sogane, which was twenty furlongs off Gabara; and by using this stratagem, I so managed myself, as not to appear to begin a civil war ,amongst them.

52. But when I was come near Sogane, I caused the multitude to make a halt, and exhorted them not to be so easily provoked to anger, and to the inflicting such punishments as could not be afterwards recalled: I also gave order, that a hundred men, who were already in years, and were principal men among them, should get themselves ready to go to the city of Jerusalem, and should .make a complaint before the people of such as raised seditions in the country. And I said to them, that" in case they be moved with what you say, you shall desire the community to write to me, and to enjoin me to continue in Galilee, and to order Jonathan and his colleagues to depart out of it." When I had suggested these instructions to them, and while they were getting themselves ready as fast as they could, I sent them on this errand the third day after they had been assembled: I also sent five hundred armed men with them [as a guard]. I then wrote to my friends in Samaria, to take care that they might safely pass through the country: for Samaria was already under the Romans, and it was absolutely necessary for those that go quickly [to Jerusalem] to pass through that country; for in that road you may, in three days' time, go from Galilee to Jerusalem. I also went myself, and conducted the old men as far as the bounds of Galilee, and set guards in the roads, that it might not be easily

known by any one that these men were gone. And when I had thus done, I went and abode at Japha.

53. Now Jonathan and his colleagues, having failed of accomplishing what they would have done against me, sent John back to Gischala, but went themselves to the city of Tiberias, expecting it would submit itself to them; and this was founded on a letter which Jesus, their then governor, had written them, promising that, if they came, the multitude would receive them, and choose to be under their government; so they went their ways with this expectation. But Silas, who, as I said, had been left curator of Tiberias by me, informed me of this, and desired me to make haste thither. Accordingly, I complied with his advice immediately, and came thither; but found myself in danger of my life, from the following occasion: Jonathan and his colleagues had been at Tiberias, and had persuaded a great many of such as had a quarrel with me to desert me; but when they heard of my coming, they were in fear for themselves, and came to me; and when they had saluted me, they said, that I was a happy man in having behaved myself so well in the government of Galilee; and they congratulated me upon the honors that were paid me: for they said that my glory was a credit to them, since they had been my teachers and fellow citizens; and they said further, that it was but just that they should prefer my friendship to them rather than John's, and that they would have immediately gone home, but that they staid that they might deliver up John into my power; and when they said this they took their oaths of it, and those such as are most tremendous amongst us, and such as I did not think fit to disbelieve. However, they desired me to lodge some where else, because the next day was the sabbath, and that it was not fit the city of Tiberias should be disturbed [on that day].

54. So I suspected nothing, and went away to Tarichese; yet did I withal leave some to make inquiry in the city how matters went, and whether any thing was said about me: I also set many persons all the way that led from Tarichese to Tiberias, that they might communicate from one to another, if they learned any news from those that were left in the city. On the next day, therefore, they all came into the Proseucha; it was a large edifice, and capable of receiving a great number of people; thither Jonathan went in, and though he durst not openly speak of a revolt, yet did he say that their city stood in need of a better governor than it then had. But Jesus, who was the ruler, made no scruple to speak out, and said openly," O fellow citizens! it is better for you to be in subjection to four than to one; and those such as are of high birth, and not without reputation for their wisdom;" and pointed to Jonathan and his colleagues. Upon his saying this, Justus came in and commended him for what he had said, and persuaded some of the people to be of his mind also. But the

multitude were not pleased with what was said, and had certainly gone into a tumult, unless the sixth hour, which was now come, had dissolved the assembly, at which hour our laws require us to go to dinner on sabbath days; so Jonathan and his colleagues put off their council till the next day, and went off without success. When I was informed of these affairs, I determined to go to the city of Tiberias in the morning. Accordingly, on the next day, about the first hour of the day, I came from Tarichee, and found the multitude already assembled in the Proseucha; but on what account they were gotten together, those that were assembled did not know. But when Jonathan and his colleagues saw me there unexpectedly, they were in disorder; after which they raised a report of their own contrivance, that Roman horsemen were seen at a place called Union, in the borders of Galilee, thirty furlongs distant from the city. Upon which report, Jonathan and his colleagues cunningly exhorted me not to neglect this matter, nor to suffer the land to be spoiled by the enemy. And this they said with a design to remove me out of the city, under the pretense of the want of extraordinary assistance, while they might dispose the city to be my enemy.

55. As for myself, although I knew of their design, yet did I comply with what they proposed, lest the people of Tiberias should have occasion to suppose that I was not careful of their security. I therefore went out; but, when I was at the place, I found not the least footsteps of any enemy, so I returned as fast as ever I could, and found the whole council assembled, and the body of the people gotten together, and Jonathan and his colleagues bringing vehement accusations against me, as one who had no concern to ease them of the burdens of war, and as one that lived luxuriously. And as they were discoursing thus, they produced four letters, as written to them from some people that lived at the borders of Galilee, imploring that they would come to their assistance, for that there was an army of Romans, both horsemen and footmen, who would come and lay waste the country on the third day; they desired them also to make haste, and not to overlook them. When the people of Tiberias heard this, they thought they spake truth, and made a clamor against me, and said I ought not to sit still, but to go away to the assistance of their countrymen. Hereupon I said (for I understood the meaning of Jonathan and his colleagues) that I was ready to comply with what they proposed, and without delay to march to the war which they spake of, yet did I advise them, at the same time, that since these letters declared that the Romans would make their assault in four several places, they should part their forces into five bodies, and make Jonathan and his colleagues generals of each body of them, because it was fit for brave men, not only to give counsel, but to take the place of

leaders, and assist their countrymen when such a necessity pressed them; for, said I, it is not possible for me to lead more than one party. This advice of mine greatly pleased the multitude; so they compelled them to go forth to the war. But their designs were put into very much disorder, because they had not done what they had designed to do, on account of my stratagem, which was opposite to their undertakings.

56. Now there was one whose name was Ananias (a wicked man he was, and very mischievous); he proposed that a general religious fast should be appointed the next day for all the people, and gave order that at the same hour they should come to the same place, without any weapons, to make it manifest before God, that while they obtained his assistance, they thought all these weapons useless. This he said, not out of piety, but that they might catch me and my friends unarmed. Now, I was hereupon forced to comply, lest I should appear to despise a proposal that tended to piety. As soon, therefore, as we were gone home, Jonathan and his colleagues wrote to John to come to them in the morning, and desiring him to come with as many soldiers as he possibly could, for that they should then be able easily to get me into their hands, and to do all they desired to do. When John had received this letter, he resolved to comply with it. As for myself, on the next day, I ordered two of the guards of my body, whom I esteemed the most courageous and most faithful, to hide daggers under their garments, and to go along with me, that we might defend ourselves, if any attack should be made upon us by our enemies. I also myself took my breastplate, and girded on my sword, so that it might be, as far as it was possible, concealed, and came into the Proseucha.

57. Now Jesus, who was the ruler, commanded that they should exclude all that came with me, for he kept the door himself, and suffered none but his friends to go in. And while we were engaged in the duties of the day, and had betaken ourselves to our prayers, Jesus got up, and inquired of me what was become of the vessels that were taken out of the king's palace, when it was burnt down [and] of that uncoined silver; and in whose possession they now were? This he said, in order to drive away time till John should come. I said that Capellus, and the ten principal men of Tiberias, had them all; and I told him that they might ask them whether I told a lie or not. And when they said they had them, he asked me, What is become of those twenty pieces of gold which thou didst receive upon the sale of a certain weight of uncoined money? I replied, that I had given them to those ambassadors of theirs, as a maintenance for them, when they were sent by them to Jerusalem. So Jonathan and his colleagues said that I had not done well to pay the ambassadors out of the public money. And when the multitude were very angry at them for this, for

they perceived the wickednes of the men, I understood that a tumult was going to arise; and being desirous to provoke the people to a greater rage against the men, I said, "But if I have not done well in paying our ambassadors out of the public stock, leave off your anger at me, for I will repay the twenty pieces of gold myself."

58. When I had said this, Jonathan and his colleagues held their peace; but the people were still more irritated against them, upon their openly showing their unjust ill-will to me. When Jesus saw this change in file people, he ordered them to depart, but desired the senate to stay; for that they could not examine things of such a nature in a tumult: and as the people were crying out that they would not leave me alone, there came one and told Jesus and his friends privately, that John and his armed men were at hand: whereupon Jonathan and his colleagues, being able to contain themselves no longer, (and perhaps the providence of God hereby procuring my deliverance, for had not this been so, I had certainly been destroyed by John,) said, "O you people of Tiberias! leave off this inquiry about the twenty pieces of gold; for Josephus hath not deserved to die for them; but he hath deserved it by his desire of tyrannizing, and by cheating the multitude of the Galileans with his speeches, in order to gain the dominion over them." When he had said this, they presently laid hands upon me, and endeavored to kill me: but as soon as those that were with me saw what they did, they drew their swords, and threatened to smite them, if they offered any violence to me. The people also took up stones, and were about to throw them at Jonathan; and so they snatched me from the violence of my enemies.

59. But as I was gone out a little way, I was just upon meeting John, who was marching with his armed men. So I was afraid of him, and turned aside, and escaped by a narrow passage to the lake, and seized on a ship, and embarked in it, and sailed over to Tarichese. So, beyond my expectation, I escaped this danger. Whereupon I presently sent for the chief of the Galileans, and told them after what manner, against all faith given, I had been very near to destruction from Jonathan and his colleagues, and the people of Tiberias. Upon which the multitude of the Galileans were very. angry, and encouraged me to delay no longer to make war upon them, but to permit them to go against John, and utterly to destroy him, as well as Jonathan and his colleagues. However, I restrained them, though they were in such a rage, and desired them to tarry a while, till we should be informed what orders those ambassadors, that were sent by them to the city of Jerusalem, should bring thence; for I told them that it was best for them to act according to their determination; where-

upon they were prevailed on. At which time, also, John, when the snares he had laid did not take effect, returned back to Gischala.

60. Now, in a few days, those ambassadors whom he had sent, came back again and informed us, that the people were greatly provoked at Ananus, and Simon the son of Gamaliel, and their friends; that, without any public determination, they had sent to Galilee, and had done their endeavors that I might be turned out of the government. The ambassadors said further, that the people were ready to burn their houses. They also brought letters, whereby the chief men of Jerusalem, at the earnest petition of the people, confirmed me in the government of Galilee, and enjoined Jonathan and his colleagues to return home quickly. When I had gotten these letters, I came to the village Arbela, where I procured an assembly of the Galileans to meet, and bid the ambassadors declare to them the anger of the people of Jerusalem at what had been done by Jonathan and his colleagues, and how much they hated their wicked doings, and how they had confirmed me in the government of their country, as also what related to the order they had in writing for Jonathan and his colleagues to return home. So I immediately sent them the letter, and bid him that carried it to inquire, as well as he could, how they intended to act [on this occasion.]

61. Now, when they had received that letter, and were thereby greatly disturbed, they sent for John, and for the senators of Tiberias, and for the principal men of the Gabarens, and proposed to hold a council, and desired them to consider what was to be done by them. However, the governors of Tiberias were greatly disposed to keep the government to themselves; for they said it was not fit to desert their city, now it was committed to their trust, and that otherwise I should not delay to fall upon them; for they pretended falsely that so I had threatened to do. Now John was not only of their opinion, but advised them, that two of them should go to accuse me before the multitude [at Jerusalem], that I do not manage the affairs of Galilee as I ought to do; and that they would easily persuade the people, because of their dignity, and because the whole multitude are very mutable. When, therefore, it appeared that John had suggested the wisest advice to them, they resolved that two of them, Jonathan and Ananias, should go to the people of Jerusalem, and the other two [Simon and Joazar] should be left behind to tarry at Tiberins. They also took along with them a hundred soldiers for their guard.

62. However, the governors of Tiberias took care to have their city secured with walls, and commanded their inhabitants to take their arms. They also sent for a great many soldiers from John, to assist them against me, if there should be occasion for them. Now John was at Gischala. Jonathan, therefore, and

those that were with him, when they were departed from Tiberias, and as soon as they were come to Dabaritta, a village that lay in the utmost parts of Galilee, in the great plain, they, about midnight, fell among the guards I had set, who both commanded them to lay aside their weapons, and kept them in bonds upon the place, as I had charged them to do. This news was written to me by Levi, who had the command of that guard committed to him by me. Hereupon I said nothing of it for two days; and, pretending to know nothing about it, I sent a message to the people of Tiberias, and advised them to lay their arms aside, and to dismiss their men, that they might go home. But, supposing that Jonathan, and those that were with him, were already arrived at Jerusalem, they made reproachful answers to me; yet was I not terrified thereby, but contrived another stratagem against them, for I did not think it agreeable with piety to kindle the fire of war against the citizens. As I was desirous to draw those men away from Tiberias, I chose out ten thousand of the best of my armed men, and divided them into three bodies, and ordered them to go privately, and lie still as an ambush, in the villages. I also led a thousand into another village, which lay indeed in the mountains, as did the others, but only four furlongs distant from Tiberias; and gave orders, that when they saw my signal, they should come down immediately, while I myself lay with my soldiers in the sight of every body. Hereupon the people of Tiberias, at the sight of me, came running out of the city perpetually, and abused me greatly. Nay, their madness was come to that height, that they made a decent bier for me, and, standing about it, they mourned over me in the way of jest and sport; and I could not but be myself in a pleasant humor upon the sight of this madness of theirs.

63. And now being desirous to catch Simon by a wile, and Joazar with him, I sent a message to them, and desired them to come a little way out of the city, and many of their friends to guard them; for I said I would come down to them, and make a league with them, and divide the government of Galilee with them. Accordingly, Simon was deluded on account of his imprudence, and out of the hopes of gain, and did not delay to come; but Joazar, suspecting snares were laid for him, staid behind. So when Simon was come out, and his friends with him, for his guard, I met him, and saluted him with great civility, and professed that I was obliged to him for his coming up to me; but a little while afterward I walked along with him as though I would say something to him by myself; and when I had drawn him a good way from his friends, I took him about the middle, and gave him to my friends that were with me, to carry him into a village; and, commanding my armed men to come down, I with them made an assault upon Tiberias. Now, as the fight grew hot on both sides,

and the soldiers belonging to Tiberias were in a fair way to conquer me, (for my armed men were already fled away,) I saw the posture of my affairs; and encouraging those that were with me, I pursued those of Tiberias, even when they were already conquerors, into the city. I also sent another band of soldiers into the city by the lake, and gave them orders to set on fire the first house they could seize upon. When this was done, the people of Tiberinas thought that their city was taken by force, and so threw down their arms for fear, and implored, they, their wives, and children, that I would spare their city. So I was over-persuaded by their entreaties, and restrained the soldiers from the vehemency with which they pursued them; while I myself, upon the coming on of the evening, returned back with my soldiers, and went to refresh myself. I also invited Simon to sup with me, and comforted him on occasion of what had happened; and I promised that I would send him safe and secure to Jerusalem, and withal would give him provisions for his journey thither.

64. But on the next day, I brought ten thousand armed men with me, and came to Tiberias. I then sent for the principal men of the multitude into the public place, and enjoined them to tell me who were the authors of the revolt; and when they told me who the men were, I sent them bound to the city Jotapata. But as to Jonathan and Ananias, I freed them from their bonds, and gave them provisions for their journey, together with Simon and Joazar, and five hundred armed men who should guard them; and so I sent them to Jerusalem. The people of Tiberias also came to me again, and desired that I would forgive them for what they had done; and they said they would amend what they had done amiss with regard to me, by their fidelity for the time to come; and they besought me to preserve what spoils remained upon the plunder of the city, for those that had lost them. Accordingly, I enjoined those that had got them, to bring them all before us; and when they did not comply for a great while, and I saw one of the soldiers that were about me with a garment on that was more splendid than ordinary, I asked him whence he had it; and when he replied that he had it out of the plunder of the city, I had him punished with stripes; and I threatened all the rest to inflict a severer punishment upon them, unless they produced before us whatsoever they had plundered; and when a great many spoils were brought together, I restored to every one of Tiberias what they claimed to be their own.

65. And now I am come to this part of my narration, I have a mind to say a few things to Justus, who hath himself written a history concerning these affairs, as also to others who profess to write history, but have little regard to truth, and are not afraid, either out of ill-will or good-will to some persons, to relate falsehoods. These men do like those who compose forged deeds and

conveyances; and because they are not brought to the like punishment with them, they have no regard to truth. When, therefore, Justus undertook to write about these facts, and about the Jewish war, that he might appear to have been an industrious man, he falsified in what he related about me, and could not speak truth even about his own country; whence it is that, being belied by him, I am under a necessity to make my defense; and so I shall say what I have concealed till now. And let no one wonder that I have not told the world these things a great while ago. For although it be necessary for an historian to write the truth, yet is such a one not bound severely to animadvert on the wickedness of certain men; not out of any favor to them, but out of an author's own moderation. How then comes it to pass, O Justus! thou most sagacious of writers, (that I may address myself to him as if he were here present,) for so thou boastest of thyself, that I and the Galileans have been the authors of that sedition which thy country engaged in, both against the Romans and against the king [Agrippa, junior] For before ever I was appointed governor of Galilee by the community of Jerusalem, both thou and all the people of Tiberias had not only taken up arms, but had made war with Decapolis of Syria. Accordingly, thou hadst ordered their villages to be burnt, and a domestic servant of thine fell in the battle. Nor is it I only who say this; but so it is written in the Commentaries of Vespasian, the emperor; as also how the inhabitants of Decapolis came clamoring to Vespasian at Ptolemais, and desired that thou, who wast the author [of that war], mightest be brought to punishment. And thou hadst certainly been punished at the command of Vespasian, had not king Agrippa, who had power given him to have thee put to death, at the earnest entreaty of his sister Bernice, changed the punishment from death into a long imprisonment. Thy political administration of affairs afterward doth also clearly discover both thy other behavior in life, and that thou wast the occasion of thy country's revolt from the Romans; plain signs of which I shall produce presently. I have also a mind to say a few things to the rest of the people of Tiberias on thy account, and to demonstrate to those that light upon this history, that you bare no good-will, neither to the Romans, nor to the king. To be sure, the greatest cities of Galilee, O Justus! were Sepphoris, and thy country Tiberias. But Sepphoris, situated in the very midst of Galilee, and having many villages about it, and able with ease to have been bold and troublesome to the Romans, if they had so pleased, yet did it resolve to continue faithful to those their masters, and at the same time excluded me out of their city, and prohibited all their citizens from joining with the Jews in the war; and, that they might be out of danger from me, they, by a wile, got leave of me to fortify their city with walls: they also, of their own accord, admitted of a garrison of Roman legions, sent them by Cestlus Gallus, who was then president of Syria, and so had me in contempt, though I was then very powerful, and all were greatly afraid of me; and at the same time that the greatest of our cities, Jerusalem, was besieged, and that temple of ours, which belonged to us all, was in danger of falling under the enemy's power, they sent no assistance thither, as not willing to have it thought they would bear arms against the Romans. But as for thy country, O Justus: situated upon the lake of Gennesareth, and distance from Hippos thirty furlongs, from Gadara sixty, and from Scythopolis, which was under the king's jurisdiction, a hundred and twenty; when there was no Jewish city near, it might easily have preserved its fidelity [to the Romans,] if it had so pleased them to do, for the city and its people had plenty of weapons. But, as thou sayest, I was then the author [of their revolts]. And pray, O Justus! who was that author afterwards? For thou knowest that I was in the power of the Romans before Jerusalem was besieged, and before the same time Jotapata was taker by force, as well as many other fortresses, and a great many of the Galileans fell in the war. It was therefore then a proper time, when you were certainly freed from any fear on my account, to throw away your weapons, and to demonstrate to the king and to the Romans, that it was not of choice, but as forced by necessity, that you fell into the war against them; but you staid till Vespasian came himself as far as your walls, with his whole army; and then you did indeed lay aside your weapons out of fear, and your city had for certain been taken by force, unless Vespasian had complied with the king's supplication for you, and had excused your madness. It was not I, therefore, who was the author of this, but your own inclinations to war. Do not you remember how often I got you under my power, and yet put none of you to death? Nay, you once fell into a tumult one against another, and slew one hundred and eighty-five of your citizens, not on account of your good-will to the king and to the Romans, but on account of your own wickedness, and this while I was besieged by the Romans in Jotapata. Nay, indeed, were there not reckoned up two thousand of the people of Tiberias during the siege of Jerusalem, some of whom were slain, and the rest caught and carried captives? But thou wilt pretend that thou didst not engage in the war, since thou didst flee to the king. Yes, indeed, thou didst flee to him; but I say it was out of fear of me. Thou sayest, indeed, that it is I who am a wicked man. But then, for what reason was it that king Agrippa, who procured thee thy life when thou wast condemned to die by Vespian, and who bestowed so much riches upon thee, did twice afterward put thee in bonds, and as often obliged thee to run away from thy country, and, when he had once ordered thee to be put to death, he granted thee a pardon at the earnest desire of Bernice? And when (after so many of thy wicked pranks) he made thee his secretary, he caught thee falsifying his epistles, and drove thee away from his sight. But I shall not inquire accurately into these matters of scandal against thee. Yet cannot I but wonder at thy impudence, when thou hast the assurance to say, that thou hast better related these affairs [of the war] than have all the others that have written about them, whilst thou didst not know what was done in Galilee; for thou wast then at Berytus with the king; nor didst thou know how much the Romans suffered at the siege of Jotapata, or what miseries they brought upon us; nor couldst thou learn by inquiry what I did during that siege myself; for all those that might afford such information were quite destroyed in that siege. But perhaps thou wilt say, thou hast written of what was done against the people of Jerusalem exactly. But how should that be? for neither wast thou concerned in that war, nor hast thou read the commentaries of Caesar; of which we have evident proof, because thou hast contradicted those commentaries of Caesar in thy history. But if thou art so hardy as to affirm, that thou hast written that history better than all the rest, why didst thou not publish thy history while the emperors Vespasian and Titus, the generals in that war, as well as king Agrippa and his family, who were men very well skilled in the learning of the Greeks, were all alive? for thou hast had it written these twenty years, and then mightest thou have had the testimony of thy accuracy. But now when these men are no longer with us, and thou thinkest thou canst not be contradicted, thou venturest to publish it. But then I was not in like manner afraid of my own writing, but I offered my books to the emperors themselves, when the facts were almost under men's eyes; for I was conscious to myself, that I had observed the truth of the facts; and as I expected to have their attestation to them, so I was not deceived in such expectation. Moreover, I immediately presented my history to many other persons, some of whom were concerned in the war, as was king Agrippa and some of his kindred. Now the emperor Titus was so desirous that the knowledge of these affairs should be taken from these books alone, that he subscribed his own hand to them, and ordered that they should be published; and for king Agrippa, he wrote me sixty-two letters, and attested to the truth of what I had therein delivered; two of which letters I have here subjoined, and thou mayst thereby know their contents: - "King Agrippa to Josephus, however, when thou comest to me, I will inform thee of a great many things which thou dost not know." So when this history was perfected, Agrippa, neither by way of flattery, which was not agreeable to him, nor by way of irony, as thou wilt say, (for he was entirely a stranger to such an evil disposition of mind,) but he wrote this by way of attestation to what was true, as all that read histories may do. And so much shall be said concerning Justus which I am obliged to add by way of digression.

66. Now, when I had settled the affairs of Tiberias, and had assembled my friends as a sanhedrim, I consulted what I should do as to John. Whereupon it appeared to be the opinion of all the Galileans, that I should arm them all, and march against John, and punish him as the author of all the disorders that had happened. Yet was not I pleased with their determination; as purposing to compose these troubles without bloodshed. Upon this I exhorted them to use the utmost care to learn the names of all that were under John; which when they had done, and I thereby was apprized who the men were, I published an edict, wherein I offered security and my right hand to such of John's party as had a mind to repent; and I allowed twenty days' time to such as would take this most advantageous course for themselves. I also threatened, that unless they threw down their arms, I would burn their houses, and expose their goods to public sale. When the men heard of this, they were in no small disorder, and deserted John; and to the number of four thousand threw down their arms, and came to me. So that no others staid with John but his own citizens, and about fifteen hundred strangers that came from the metropolis of Tyre; and when John saw that he had been outwitted by my stratagem, he continued afterward in his own country, and was in great fear of me.

67. But about this time it was that the people of Sepphoris grew insolent, and took up arms, out of a confidence they had in the strength of their walls, and because they saw me engaged in other affairs also. So they sent to Cestius Gallus, who was president of Syria, and desired that he would either come quickly to them, and take their city under his protection, or send them a garrison. Accordingly, Gallus promised them to come, but did not send word when he would come: and when I had learned so much, I took the soldiers that were with me, and made an assault upon the people of Sepphoris, and took the city by force. The Galileans took this opportunity, as thinking they had now a proper time for showing their hatred to them, since they bore ill-will to that city also. They then exerted themselves, as if they would destroy them all utterly, with those that sojourned there also. So they ran upon them, and set their houses on fire, as finding them without inhabitants; for the men, out of fear, ran together to the citadel. So the Galileans carried off every thing, and omitted no kind of desolation which they could bring upon their countrymen. When I saw this, I was exceedingly troubled at it, and commanded them to leave off, and put them in mind that it was not agreeable to piety to do such things to their countrymen: but since they neither would hearken to what I exhorted, nor to what I commanded them to do, (for the hatred they

bore to the people there was too hard for my exhortations to them,) I bade those my friends, who were most faithful to me, and were about me, to give on reports, as if the Romans were falling upon the other part of the city with a great army; and this I did, that, by such a report being spread abroad, I might restrain the violence of the Galileans, and preserve the city of Sepphoris. And at length this stratagem had its effect; for, upon hearing this report, they were in fear for themselves, and so they left off plundering and ran away; and this more especially, because they saw me, their general, do the same also; for, that I might cause this report to be believed, I pretended to be in fear as well as they. Thus were the inhabitants of Sepphoris unexpectedly preserved by this contrivance of mine.

68. Nay, indeed, Tiberias had like to have been plundered by the Galileans also upon the following occasion: - The chief men of the senate wrote to the king, and desired that he would come to them, and take possession of their city. The king promised to come, and wrote a letter in answer to theirs, and gave it to one of his bed-chamber, whose name was Crispus, and who was by birth a Jew, to carry it to Tiberias. When the Galileans knew that this man carried such a letter, they caught him, and brought him to me; but as soon as the whole multitude heard of it, they were enraged, and betook themselves to their arms. So a great many of them together from all quarters the next day, and came to the city Asochis, where I then lodged, and made heavy clamors, and called the city of Tiberias a traitor to them, and a friend to the king; and desired leave of me to go down and utterly destroy it; for they bore the like ill-will to the people of Tiberias, as they did to those of Sepphoris.

69. When I heard this, I was in doubt what to do, and hesitated by what means I might deliver Tiberias from the rage of the Galileans; for I could not deny that those of Tiborias had written to the king, and invited him to come to them; for his letters to them, in answer thereto, would fully prove the truth of that. So I sat a long time musing with myself, and then said to them, "I know well enough that the people of Tiberias have offended; nor shall I forbid you to plunder the city. However, such things ought to be done with discretion; for they of Tiberias have not been the only betrayers of our liberty, but many of the most eminent patriots of the Galileans, as they pretended to be, have done the same. Tarry therefore till I shall thoroughly find out those authors of our danger, and then you shall have them all at once under your power, with all such as you shall yourselves bring in also." Upon my saying this, I pacifie the multitude, and they left off their anger, and went their ways; and I gave orders that he who brought the king's letters should be put into bonds; but in a few days I pretended that I was obliged, by a necessary affair of

my own, to out of the kingdom. I then called Crispus privately, and ordered him to make the soldier that kept him drunk, and to run away to the king. So when Tiberias was in danger of being utterly destroyed a second time, it escaped the danger by my skillful management, and the care that I had for its preservation.

70. About this time it was that Justus, the son of Pistus, without my knowledge, ran away to the king; the occasion of which I will here relate. Upon the beginning of the war between the Jews and Romans, the people of Tiberias resolved to submit to the king, and not to revolt from the Romans; while Justus tried to persuade them to betake themselves to their arms, as being himself desirous of innovations, and having hopes of obtaining the government of Galilee, as well as of his own country [Tiberias] also. Yet did he not obtain what he hoped for, because the Galileans bore ill-will to those of Tiberias, and this on account of their anger at what miseries they had suffered from them before the war; thence it was that they would not endure that Justus should be their governor. I myself also, who had been intrusted by the community of Jerusalem with the government of Galilee, did frequently come to that degree of rage at Justus, that I had almost resolved to kill him, as not able to bear his mischievous disposition. He was therefore much afraid of me, lest at length my passion should come to extremity; so he went to the king, as supposing that he would dwell better and more safely with him.

71. Now, when the people of Sepphoris had, in so surprising a manner, escaped their first danger, they sent to Cestius Gallus, and desired him to come to them immediately, and take possession of their city, or else to send forces sufficient to repress all their enemies' incursions upon them; and at the last they did prevail with Gallus to send them a considerable army, both of horse and foot, which came in the night time, and which they admitted into the city. But when the country round about it was harassed by the Roman army, I took those soldiers that were about me, and came to Garisme, where I cast up a bank, a good way off the city Sepphoris; and when I was at twenty furlongs distance, I came upon it by night, and made an assault upon its walls with my forces; and when I had ordered a considerable number of my soldiers to scale them with ladders, I became master of the greatest part of the city. But soon after, our unacquaintedness with the places forced us to retire, after we had killed twelve of the Roman footmen, and two horsemen, and a few of the people of Sepphoris, with the loss of only a single man of our own. And when it afterwards came to a battle in the plain against the horsemen, and we had undergone the dangers of it courageously for a long time, we were beaten; for upon the Romans encompassing me about, my soldiers were afraid, and fell

back. There fell in that battle one of those that had been intrusted to guard my body; his name was Justus, who at this time had the same post with the king. At the same time also there came forces, both horsemen and footmen, from the king, and Sylla their commander, who was the captain of his guard: this Sylla pitched his camp at five furlongs' distance from Julias, and set a guard upon the roads, both that which led to Cana, and that which led to the fortress Gamala, that he might hinder their inhabitants from getting provisions out of Galilee.

72. As soon as I had gotten intelligence of this, I sent two thousand armed men, and a captain over them, whose name was Jeremiah, who raised a bank a furlong off Julias, near to the river Jordan, and did no more than skirmish with the enemy; till I took three thousand soldiers myself, and came to them. But on the next day, when I had laid an ambush in a certain valley, not far from the banks, I provoked those that belonged to the king to come to a battle, and gave orders to my own soldiers to turn their backs upon them, until they should have drawn the enemy away from their camp, and brought them out into the field, which was done accordingly; for Sylla, supposing that our party did really run away, was ready to pursue them, when our soldiers that lay in ambush took them on their backs, and put them all into great disorder. I also immediately made a sudden turn with my own forces, and met those of the king's party, and put them to flight. And I had performed great things that day, if a certain fate had not been my hinderance; for the horse on which I rode, and upon whose back I fought, fell into a quagmire, and threw me on the ground, and I was bruised on my wrist, and carried into a village named Cepharnome, or Capernaum. When my soldiers heard of this, they were afraid I had been worse hurt than I was; and so they did not go on with their pursuit any further, but returned in very great concern for me. I therefore sent for the physicians, and while I was under their hands, I continued feverish that day; and as the physicians directed, I was that night removed to Taricheee.

73. When Sylla and his party were informed what happened to me, they took courage again; and understanding that the watch was negligently kept in our camp, they by night placed a body of horsemen in ambush beyond Jordan, and when it was day they provoked us to fight; and as we did not refuse it, but came into the plain, their horsemen appeared out of that ambush in which they had lain, and put our men into disorder, and made them run away; so they slew six men of our side. Yet did they not go off with the victory at last; for when they heard that some armed men were sailed from Taricheae to Juli, they were afraid, and retired.

74. It was not now long before Vespasian came to Tyre, and king Agrippa with him; but the Tyrians began to speak reproachfully of the king, and called him an enemy to the Romans. For they said that Philip, the general of his army, had betrayed the royal palace and the Roman forces that were in Jerusalem, and that it was done by his command. When Vespasian heard of this report, he rebuked the Tyrians for abusing a man who was both a king and a friend to the Romans; but he exhorted the king to send Philip to Rome, to answer for what he had done before Nero. But when Philip was sent thither, he did not come into the sight of Nero, for he found him very near death, on account of the troubles that then happened, and a civil war; and so he returned to the king. But when Vespasian was come to Ptolemais, the chief men of Decapolis of Syria made a clamor against Justus of Tiberias, because he had set their villages on fire: so Vespasian delivered him to the king, to he put to death by those under the king's jurisdiction; yet did the king only put him into bonds, and concealed what he had done from Vespasian, as I have before related. But the people of Sepphoris met Vespasian, and saluted him, and had forces sent him, with Placidus their commander: he also went up with them, as I also followed them, till Vespasian came into Galilee. As to which coming of his, and after what manner it was ordered, and how he fought his first battle with me near the village Taricheae, and how from thence they went to Jotapata, and how I was taken alive, and bound, and how I was afterward loosed, with all that was done by me in the Jewish war, and during the siege of Jerusalem, I have accurately related them in the books concerning the War of the Jews. However, it will, I think, he fit for me to add now an account of those actions of my life which I have not related in that book of the Jewish war.

75. For when the siege of Jotapata was over, and I was among the Romans, I was kept with much Care, by means of the great respect that Vespasian showed me. Moreover, at his command, I married a virgin, who was from among the captives of that country yet did she not live with me long, but was divorced, upon my being freed from my bonds, and my going to Alexandria. However, I married another wife at Alexandria, and was thence sent, together with Titus, to the siege of Jerusalem, and was frequently in danger of being put to death; while both the Jews were very desirous to get me under their power, in order to haw me punished. And the Romans also, whenever they were beaten, supposed that it was occasioned by my treachery, and made continual clamors to the emperors, and desired that they would bring me to punishment, as a traitor to them: but Titus Caesar was well acquainted with the uncertain fortune of war, and returned no answer to the soldiers' vehement solicitations against me. Moreover, when the city Jerusalem was taken by force, Titus

Caesar persuaded me frequently to take whatsoever I would of the ruins of my country; and did that he gave me leave so to do. But when my country was destroyed, I thought nothing else to be of any value, which I could take and keep as a comfort under my calamities; so I made this request to Titus, that my family might have their liberty: I had also the holy books by Titus's concession. Nor was it long after that I asked of him the life of my brother, and of fifty friends with him, and was not denied. When I also went once to the temple, by the permission of Titus, where there were a great multitude of captive women and children, I got all those that I remembered as among my own friends and acquaintances to be set free, being in number about one hundred and ninety; and so I delivered them without their paying any price of redemption, and restored them to their former fortune. And when I was sent by Titus Caesar with Cerealins, and a thousand horsemen, to a certain village called Thecoa, in order to know whether it were a place fit for a camp, as I came back, I saw many captives crucified, and remembered three of them as my former acquaintance. I was very sorry at this in my mind, and went with tears in my eyes to Titus, and told him of them; so he immediately commanded them to be taken down, and to have the greatest care taken of them, in order to their recovery; yet two of them died under the physician's hands, while the third recovered.

76. But when Titus had composed the troubles in Judea, and conjectured that the lands which I had in Judea would bring me no profit, because a garrison to guard the country was afterward to pitch there, he gave me another country in the plain. And when he was going away to Rome, he made choice of me to sail along with him, and paid me great respect: and when we were come to Rome, I had great care taken of me by Vespasian; for he gave me an apartment in his own house, which he lived in before he came to the empire. He also honored me with the privilege of a Roman citizen, and gave me an annual pension; and continued to respect me to the end of his life, without any abatement of his kindness to me; which very thing made me envied, and brought me into danger; for a certain Jew, whose name was Jonathan, who had raised a tumult in Cyrene, and had persuaded two thousand men of that country to join with him, was the occasion of their ruin. But when he was bound by the governor of that country, and sent to the emperor, he told him that I had sent him both weapons and money. However, he could not conceal his being a liar from Vespasian, who condemned him to die; according to which sentence he was put to death. Nay, after that, when those that envied my good fortune did frequently bring accusations against me, by God's providence I escaped them all. I also received from Vespasian no small quantity of

land, as a free gift, in Judea; about which time I divorced my wife also, as not pleased with her behavior, though not till she had been the mother of three children, two of whom are dead, and one whom I named Hyrcanus, is alive. After this I married a wife who had lived at Crete, but a Jewess by birth: a woman she was of eminent parents, and such as were the most illustrious in all the country, and whose character was beyond that of most other women, as her future life did demonstrate. By her I had two sons; the elder's name was Justus, and the next Simonides, who was also named Agrippa. And these were the circumstances of my domestic affairs. However, the kindness of the emperor to me continued still the same; for when Vespasian was dead, Titus, who succeeded him in the government, kept up the same respect for me which I had from his father; and when I had frequent accusations laid against me, he would not believe them. And Domitian, who succeeded, still augmented his respects to me; for he punished those Jews that were my accusers, and gave command that a servant of mine, who was a eunuch, and my accuser, should be punished. He also made that country I had in Judea tax free, which is a mark of the greatest honor to him who hath it; nay, Domitia, the wife of Caesar, continued to do me kindnesses. And this is the account of the actions of my whole life; and let others judge of my character by them as they please. But to thee, O Epaphroditus, thou most excellent of men! do I dedicate all this treatise of our Antiquities; and so, for the present, I here conclude the whole.

13641636R00030

Printed in Great Britain
by Amazon.co.uk, Ltd.,
Marston Gate.

THE family from which I am derived is not an ignoble one, but hath descended all along from the priests; and as nobility among several people is of a different origin, so with us to be of the sacerdotal dignity, is an indication of the splendor of a family. Now, I am not only sprung from a sacerdotal family in general, but from the first of the twenty-four courses; and as among us there is not only a considerable difference between one family of each course and another, I am of the chief family of that first course also; nay, further, by my mother I am of the royal blood; for the children of Asamoneus, from whom that family was derived, had both the office of the high priesthood, and the dignity of a king, for a long time together. I will accordingly set down my progenitors in order.

ISBN 9781785167331

90000 >

9 781785 167331